Table of Co

Introduction 2

Chapter 1: Understanding Your Cat 8

Chapter 2: Basic Training Techniques 14

Chapter 3: Advanced Training Techniques 20

Chapter 4: Dealing with Behavioral Problems ... 27

Chapter 5: Environmental Enrichment for Cats . 34

Chapter 6: Health and Safety Considerations 40

Chapter7: Conclusion 47

Introduction

If you are a cat lover, you may have wondered if you can train your feline friend to do tricks, obey commands, or simply behave better. The answer is a resounding YES! With the right approach and the patience to go along with it, you can train your cat to be a well-behaved and obedient pet. In this guide, we will cover the benefits of training your cat, common misconceptions about cat training, and the principles of positive reinforcement.

The Benefits of Training Your Cat:

Many people believe that cats are independent and aloof animals that cannot be trained. However, training your cat can bring several benefits, including:

Strengthening Your Bond: Training your cat can help to build a stronger bond between you and your feline friend. It can help your cat to understand your expectations, and it can help you to understand your cat's behavior and personality.

Reducing Problem Behavior: Training can help to reduce problem behavior such as scratching, biting, or urinating outside the litter box. Training can also help to teach your cat to come when called, sit, stay, and perform other basic commands.

Providing Mental Stimulation: Training provides mental stimulation for your cat, which can help to prevent boredom and reduce stress. This is especially important for indoor cats, who may not have as many opportunities for physical exercise and play.

Enabling Fun Activities: Training your cat can open up new and fun activities for you and your pet to enjoy together. You can teach your cat to play games, perform tricks, and even go for walks on a leash.

The Common Misconceptions About Cat Training:

There are several misconceptions about training cats that can deter people from trying it. Some of the most common misconceptions include:

Cats Cannot Be Trained: While it is true that cats are independent creatures, they are also intelligent and capable of learning. With the right approach and a lot of patience, you can train your cat to do almost anything that a dog can do.

Training is Punitive: Many people believe that training involves punishment or negative reinforcement. However, training should always be based on positive reinforcement, which involves rewarding good behavior rather than punishing bad behavior.

Training is Time-Consuming: While it is true that training your cat requires time and effort, it is not necessarily a time-consuming process. With regular and consistent training sessions, you can teach your cat new behaviors in a relatively short amount of time.

Cats Will Only Learn What They Want to Learn: This is not entirely true. While cats are independent and will only do what they want to do, they can be motivated to learn new behaviors if they are rewarded for doing so.

The Principles of Positive Reinforcement:

Positive reinforcement is the most effective and humane approach to cat training. It involves rewarding your cat for good behavior rather than punishing bad behavior. Here are the basic principles of positive reinforcement:

Rewards: Rewards can include treats, praise, petting, or playtime. The reward should be something that your cat enjoys and finds motivating.

Timing: Timing is crucial when using positive reinforcement. You should always reward your cat immediately after he or she exhibits the desired behavior. This helps your cat to associate the behavior with the reward.

Consistency: Consistency is essential in training your cat. You should always use the same commands and rewards and be consistent in your training sessions. This helps your cat to understand what is expected of him or her.

Patience: Patience is key when training your cat. You should expect that your cat will make mistakes and take longer to learn some behaviors than others. The key is to remain patient and consistent in your training.

Conclusion:

In conclusion, training your cat is not only possible, but it can also be a rewarding and beneficial experience for both you and your pet. By using positive reinforcement and being patient and consistent in your training, you can teach your cat new behaviors, reduce problem behavior, and provide mental stimulation.

It is important to remember that training your cat requires time and effort, and you should not expect overnight results. It is also important to consider your cat's individual personality and behavior when approaching training. Some cats may be more receptive to training than others, and some may require a different approach or more patience.

Overall, training your cat can be a fun and rewarding experience for both you and your pet. By following the principles of positive reinforcement and being patient and consistent in your training, you can build a stronger bond with your cat and create a well-behaved and happy pet.

Chapter 1: Understanding Your Cat

Cats are fascinating creatures that have been domesticated for thousands of years. They have an independent nature and a unique set of behaviors that make them different from other pets. As a cat owner, it's important to understand your cat's natural behavior, body language, and vocalization in order to build a strong relationship with your feline friend. In this chapter, we will discuss the natural behavior of cats, how to interpret their body language, and how to identify your cat's personality.

The Natural Behavior of Cats

Cats are predators by nature and have a keen sense of sight, hearing, and smell. They have evolved over time to become solitary hunters that are efficient at catching their prey. In the wild, cats hunt small animals such as birds, rodents, and insects. They are also territorial animals that mark their territory by rubbing their scent on objects or spraying urine.

Domesticated cats have retained many of their natural behaviors. They are still hunters at heart, and will often play with toys or hunt imaginary prey. They also have a strong desire to scratch, which is a natural behavior that helps them keep their claws sharp and mark their territory.

Understanding Body Language and Vocalization

Cats communicate in a variety of ways, including body language, vocalization, and scent marking. By understanding your cat's body language and vocalization, you can learn how they are feeling and what they want. Here are some common body language cues to look for:

Ears: When a cat's ears are facing forward, they are alert and interested in their surroundings. When their ears are flattened back, it indicates that they are scared or angry.

Eyes: A cat's eyes can convey a lot of information. Dilated pupils indicate that they are either excited or scared, while narrow pupils suggest they are feeling threatened or defensive.

Tail: A cat's tail can indicate their mood. A straight and upright tail suggests they are happy, while a puffed up tail indicates they are scared or angry.

Posture: The way a cat is standing or sitting can also indicate their mood. A cat that is crouching low to the ground is likely scared or defensive, while a cat that is lying on their back is feeling relaxed and comfortable.

In addition to body language, cats also communicate through vocalization. They can meow, hiss, growl, and even purr. A cat's meow can convey a variety of messages, such as hunger, attention, or even greeting. A hiss or growl is a sign of aggression or fear, while a purr is a sign of contentment.

Identifying Your Cat's Personality

Just like humans, cats have unique personalities. Some cats are outgoing and friendly, while others are shy and reserved. It's important to identify your cat's personality so that you can understand their behavior and provide the best care possible.

One way to identify your cat's personality is to observe their behavior. Do they enjoy being around people or do they prefer to be alone? Are they curious and adventurous or do they prefer to stay in one place? By paying attention to your cat's behavior, you can start to identify their likes and dislikes.

Another way to identify your cat's personality is to play with them. Some cats are playful and enjoy chasing toys, while others prefer to lounge and nap. By playing with your cat, you can identify their favorite toys and activities.

It's also important to consider your cat's breed and age when identifying their personality. Some breeds, such as Siamese and Bengal cats, are known for being vocal and energetic, while others, such as Persians, are known for being more relaxed and laid back. Similarly, kittens are often more active and curious, while older cats are more mellow and enjoy quiet time.

Understanding your cat's personality can help you create a stronger bond with them, and also provide the best care possible. Knowing what they like and dislike can help you choose the right toys, treats, and activities to keep them happy and healthy.

It's also important to keep in mind that your cat's personality can change over time. As they grow and age, they may become more or less social, or may develop new likes and dislikes. By staying attuned to your cat's behavior and needs, you can continue to build a strong relationship with them over time.

Conclusion

Understanding your cat's natural behavior, body language, and personality is essential to building a strong relationship with your feline friend. By paying attention to your cat's behavior and needs, you can provide the best care possible and create a happy and healthy home for them. Remember to observe their body language and vocalization, identify their personality, and adjust your care accordingly as they grow and change over time. With patience and understanding, you can create a lifelong bond with your beloved feline companion.

Chapter 2: Basic Training Techniques

Training a cat can be an exciting and fulfilling process for both you and your furry companion. However, it is essential to start with the basics before moving on to more advanced training. In this chapter, we will be discussing some of the fundamental training techniques, including teaching your cat to come when called, litter box training, and training your cat to use a scratching post.

Teaching your cat to come when called:

Teaching your cat to come when called is a valuable skill that can be helpful in a variety of situations. For example, if your cat has escaped outside or is hiding in a difficult-to-reach area of your home, being able to call them back can be incredibly useful.

Here are the steps to follow when teaching your cat to come when called:

Choose a sound: Start by selecting a particular sound that your cat will associate with coming to you. This sound could be a specific word, a whistle, or a clicker.

Reinforce the sound: Once you have chosen the sound, use it every time you feed your cat or give them a treat. This will help your cat associate the sound with something positive.

Call your cat: When your cat is in a different room or a short distance away, use the chosen sound and call your cat. When your cat comes to you, reward them with a treat or praise.

Practice: Practice this training exercise regularly, starting with short distances and gradually increasing the distance. Be patient and consistent, and soon, your cat will learn to come when called.

Litter box training:

Litter box training is one of the most crucial training exercises for a cat owner. It is essential to teach your cat to use the litter box as soon as possible to avoid any unwanted accidents around your home.

Here are the steps to follow when litter box training your cat:

Choose the right litter box: There are many types of litter boxes available, including open or covered, large or small, and with or without a hood. Choose the litter box that best suits your cat's needs and preferences.

Choose the right litter: There are different types of litter available, including clay, silica, and biodegradable. Experiment with different types to see which one your cat prefers.

Show your cat the litter box: When you first bring your cat home, show them where the litter box is located. You may need to physically place your cat in the litter box to get them used to it.

Reinforce positive behavior: When your cat uses the litter box, reward them with praise or a treat. This positive reinforcement will help your cat associate using the litter box with something positive.

Clean the litter box regularly: Clean the litter box at least once a day, removing any waste and replacing the litter as needed. This will help keep the litter box clean and fresh for your cat.

Training your cat to use a scratching post:

Cats naturally scratch to stretch their muscles and mark their territory. However, this behavior can be destructive to furniture and other household items. Training your cat to use a scratching post is an effective way to redirect this behavior.

Here are the steps to follow when training your cat to use a scratching post:

Choose the right scratching post: There are different types of scratching posts available, including vertical, horizontal, and angled. Choose the type of scratching post that your cat prefers.

Place the scratching post in a prominent location: Put the scratching post in an area of your home where your cat spends most of their time. This will help encourage them to use it.

Reinforce positive behavior: When your cat uses the scratching post, reward them with praise or a treat. This positive reinforcement will help your cat associate using the scratching post with something positive.

Encourage your cat to use the scratching post: Initially, your cat may be hesitant to use the scratching post. You can encourage them by gently placing their paws on the post and rewarding them when they scratch it.

Discourage unwanted behavior: If you catch your cat scratching furniture or other household items, gently redirect them to the scratching post. Never punish your cat for unwanted behavior, as this can cause them to become fearful or aggressive.

Trim your cat's nails: Regularly trimming your cat's nails can help prevent damage to furniture and other household items. Use sharp, high-quality clippers and be careful not to cut the quick.

Training your cat may take time and patience, but it is worth the effort. Remember to use positive reinforcement techniques and avoid punishment, as this can cause your cat to become fearful or aggressive. With consistent training, your cat will learn to come when called, use the litter box, and use the scratching post, leading to a happier and healthier relationship between you and your furry friend.

Chapter 3: Advanced Training Techniques

Congratulations on mastering the basic training techniques for your feline friend. You and your cat have established a solid foundation for a strong bond and a harmonious living together. As you become more confident in your training abilities, you might be interested in exploring advanced training techniques that will make your cat stand out and impress your friends and family.

In this chapter, we will discuss three advanced training techniques: clicker training, teaching your cat to walk on a leash, and training your cat to perform tricks. These techniques require more patience, persistence, and creativity. However, the rewards are worth it, as you and your cat will experience a sense of accomplishment and joy.

Clicker Training

Clicker training is a popular technique used to train many animals, including cats, dogs, horses, and dolphins. It involves using a small handheld device that makes a distinctive clicking sound when pressed. The clicker serves as a bridge between the behavior you want to reinforce and the reward that follows.

Before you start clicker training, you need to select a reward that your cat finds highly desirable, such as a small piece of tuna, chicken, or catnip. You also need to find a quiet and distraction-free environment where you and your cat can focus on the training.

The first step in clicker training is to introduce the clicker to your cat. You can do this by clicking the device and immediately offering the reward. Repeat this several times until your cat associates the clicking sound with the reward.

Once your cat understands the association, you can start teaching a behavior by using a command or a gesture. For example, you can say "sit" or make a hand gesture that signals your cat to sit. As soon as your cat performs the behavior, click the clicker and offer the reward. Repeat this several times until your cat responds to the command or gesture without the reward.

Clicker training is useful for teaching a wide range of behaviors, such as jumping, rolling over, playing dead, and high-fiving. The key is to break down the behavior into small and manageable steps and reinforce each step with a click and a reward. As your cat becomes more proficient, you can increase the complexity of the behavior and the duration of the performance.

Teaching Your Cat to Walk on a Leash

While it's common to see dogs being walked on a leash, it's not as common to see cats being walked. However, if you're interested in taking your cat for a walk, you can train your cat to walk on a leash.

The first step in leash training is to get your cat comfortable wearing a harness. A harness is a safer and more comfortable alternative to a collar, as it distributes the pressure evenly around the body, rather than the neck. Choose a harness that fits your cat snugly but not too tight. You can put the harness on your cat for short periods, gradually increasing the duration. Make sure your cat is relaxed and not agitated or anxious.

Once your cat is comfortable wearing the harness, you can attach the leash and start training your cat to walk on the leash. It's essential to choose a quiet and safe outdoor area, such as a backyard or a park, where your cat can explore without distractions or dangers.

The first few times you take your cat outside on the leash, let your cat explore and sniff around without tugging or pulling on the leash. Gradually introduce some gentle guidance, by using a treat or a toy to lure your cat to walk in a specific direction. Praise your cat and offer a reward for every successful step.

As your cat becomes more comfortable with the leash and the environment, you can increase the distance and the duration of the walks. It's essential to keep your cat safe from cars, dogs, and other hazards and to avoid overstimulation or exhaustion. Watch for signs of fatigue, such as heavy panting, drooling, or lethargy, and stop the walk if necessary.

Leash training requires patience and practice, as cats have a strong instinct to explore and wander. However, it can be a great way to bond with your cat and provide mental and physical stimulation.

Training Your Cat to Perform Tricks

Teaching your cat to perform tricks is a fun and challenging way to showcase your cat's intelligence and personality. However, not all cats are willing or capable of learning tricks, and it's important to respect your cat's natural abilities and limitations.

Before you start training your cat to perform tricks, you need to choose a reward that your cat finds highly motivating and exclusive to the training sessions. You also need to choose a quiet and distraction-free environment where you and your cat can focus on the training.

The first step in trick training is to choose a behavior that your cat can perform naturally, such as jumping, scratching, or vocalizing. Once you've identified the behavior, you need to shape it into a specific trick, such as jumping through a hoop, scratching on command, or meowing on cue.

Shaping a behavior involves breaking it down into small and manageable steps and rewarding each step with the clicker and the reward. For example, if you want to teach your cat to jump through a hoop, you can start by rewarding your cat for approaching the hoop, then for touching the hoop, then for jumping over the hoop. Gradually, you can increase the height and the distance of the hoop and the complexity of the trick.

It's important to keep the training sessions short and positive, and to avoid pushing your cat beyond its limits. If your cat shows signs of frustration, stress, or boredom, take a break and resume later. Remember to praise your cat for every effort and to celebrate every success.

Conclusion

Clicker training, leash training, and trick training are advanced techniques that require time, effort, and creativity. However, they can be highly rewarding and enriching for both you and your cat. Before you start training, make sure you and your cat are in good health and in the right mood for training. Choose the right reward and the right environment, and be patient and persistent in your training. Remember that every cat has its unique personality and learning style, and that it's important to respect and appreciate your cat's natural abilities and limitations.

Chapter 4: Dealing with Behavioral Problems

Behavioral problems can be one of the biggest challenges when it comes to training a cat. Cats are known for their independent nature and can often exhibit unwanted behaviors that can be frustrating for their owners. In this chapter, we will cover three common behavioral problems: aggression towards people or other pets, scratching furniture, and urine marking or other litter box issues. We will discuss the causes of these behaviors, how to prevent them, and how to address them when they occur.

Aggression towards people or other pets

Aggression towards people or other pets can be a serious problem that requires immediate attention. Cats can become aggressive for a variety of reasons, including fear, territoriality, and overstimulation. It is important to identify the cause of the aggression and address it appropriately.

If your cat is showing signs of aggression towards people or other pets, the first step is to consult with your veterinarian to rule out any medical conditions that could be causing the behavior. If your cat is healthy, the next step is to identify the triggers that are causing the aggression. Common triggers include loud noises, sudden movements, and unfamiliar people or animals.

Preventing aggression towards people or other pets requires a multi-faceted approach. One of the most effective ways to prevent aggression is to provide your cat with plenty of mental and physical stimulation. This can include providing toys, scratching posts, and opportunities for play and exploration. Additionally, providing your cat with a quiet and safe space to retreat to can help reduce stress and anxiety.

When it comes to addressing aggressive behavior, the first step is to remove the cat from the situation that is causing the aggression. This may mean separating your cat from other pets or removing your cat from a room with loud noises or unfamiliar people. It is important not to punish your cat for aggressive behavior, as this can cause more stress and anxiety and make the behavior worse. Instead, provide positive reinforcement for good behavior and seek the advice of a professional if the behavior persists.

Scratching furniture or other unwanted behavior

Cats have a natural instinct to scratch, which can be problematic when they choose to scratch furniture or other household items. While it can be frustrating to deal with, it is important to remember that scratching is a natural behavior that cats use to mark their territory and maintain their claws.

The first step in preventing unwanted scratching is to provide your cat with a variety of scratching surfaces. This can include scratching posts, mats, and boards. It is important to provide scratching surfaces that are sturdy and tall enough for your cat to stretch out on. Additionally, providing your cat with plenty of mental and physical stimulation can help reduce the desire to scratch.

If your cat is already scratching furniture or other household items, there are a few ways to address the behavior. One effective method is to cover the item with a material that is unappealing to your cat, such as double-sided tape or aluminum foil. Additionally, providing your cat with an alternative scratching surface and rewarding good behavior can help reduce unwanted scratching.

Urine marking or other litter box issues

One of the most common behavioral problems in cats is litter box issues, including urine marking and inappropriate elimination. These behaviors can be caused by a variety of factors, including stress, anxiety, and medical conditions.

The first step in addressing litter box issues is to consult with your veterinarian to rule out any medical conditions that could be causing the behavior. If your cat is healthy, the next step is to identify the cause of the behavior. Common causes of litter box issues include stress, anxiety, and environmental factors such as the location and cleanliness of the litter box.

Preventing litter box issues requires a multi-faceted approach. This can include providing multiple litter boxes in different locations, keeping the litter box clean and well-maintained, and providing your cat with a quiet and safe space to use the litter box. Additionally, providing mental and physical stimulation can help reduce stress and anxiety.

If your cat is already exhibiting litter box issues, there are a few ways to address the behavior. One effective method is to provide your cat with multiple litter boxes in different locations, each with a different type of litter. This can help your cat find the litter box that they are most comfortable using. Additionally, providing positive reinforcement for good litter box behavior can help encourage your cat to use the litter box consistently.

If your cat is urine marking, it is important to address the behavior immediately. This can be a sign of stress or anxiety, and can also be a sign of territorial behavior. One effective method for addressing urine marking is to clean the affected area with an enzymatic cleaner to eliminate the odor. Additionally, providing your cat with a safe and comfortable space to retreat to can help reduce stress and anxiety.

In some cases, litter box issues can be difficult to address and may require the assistance of a professional. A veterinary behaviorist or certified cat behavior consultant can help identify the cause of the behavior and provide recommendations for addressing the issue.

Conclusion

Dealing with behavioral problems in cats can be a challenge, but with patience and persistence, it is possible to address and prevent unwanted behaviors. The key to success is identifying the cause of the behavior and addressing it appropriately. Providing your cat with plenty of mental and physical stimulation, a safe and comfortable environment, and positive reinforcement for good behavior can go a long way in preventing and addressing behavioral problems in cats.

Chapter 5: Environmental Enrichment for Cats

Cats are curious creatures, and they need an environment that stimulates them mentally and physically. As pet owners, it's our responsibility to provide our feline friends with a healthy, safe, and enriching environment. In this chapter, we'll explore how to create a stimulating environment for your cat, provide mental and physical stimulation, and choose the right toys and accessories.

Creating a Stimulating Environment for Your Cat

Cats are natural explorers, and they love to roam around and discover new things. A stimulating environment for your cat means an environment that offers opportunities for exploration, play, and rest. Below are some ways to create a stimulating environment for your cat.

Vertical Space

Cats are climbers, and they love to be up high. Providing vertical space is crucial for a stimulating environment. You can achieve this by adding shelves or cat trees, where your cat can climb, perch, and observe its surroundings. Vertical space not only provides a physical challenge for your cat but also gives them a sense of security and control.

Hiding Spots

Cats love to hide and feel safe. Adding hiding spots to your cat's environment can help reduce stress and provide a sense of security. You can create hiding spots by placing boxes, tunnels, or baskets in different areas of your home.

Windows

Cats love to look outside and observe the world. Providing a window perch can give your cat a sense of connection to the outdoors, as well as mental stimulation. A window perch can also provide an opportunity for your cat to soak up some sunlight, which is beneficial for their health.

Providing Mental and Physical Stimulation

Cats need both mental and physical stimulation to maintain their health and wellbeing. Mental stimulation keeps your cat's mind active, while physical stimulation keeps their body fit and healthy. Here are some ways to provide mental and physical stimulation for your cat.

Interactive Toys

Interactive toys are a great way to provide mental and physical stimulation for your cat. Toys that require your cat to chase, pounce, and swat can help keep your cat active and engaged. Some examples of interactive toys include puzzle feeders, balls, and wand toys.

Scratching Posts

Cats have a natural instinct to scratch, and providing a scratching post can help keep your cat's claws healthy and sharp. Scratching posts also provide a physical challenge and mental stimulation. You can choose a scratching post made of different materials, such as carpet, sisal, or cardboard.

Playtime

Playtime is essential for your cat's physical and mental health. Playing with your cat can help build a bond between you and your feline friend. You can use a laser pointer, wand toys, or other interactive toys during playtime. It's also important to provide a variety of toys and rotate them regularly to keep your cat engaged.

Choosing the Right Toys and Accessories

Choosing the right toys and accessories for your cat can be overwhelming. There are so many options available, and it's important to choose toys that are safe, durable, and appropriate for your cat's age and personality. Here are some tips for choosing the right toys and accessories for your cat.

Safety First

Your cat's safety should always come first. Make sure to choose toys that are free from small parts, toxic materials, or sharp edges that can harm your cat. Avoid toys with strings, ribbons, or small balls that your cat can swallow.

Durability

Cats love to play rough, and their toys should be able to withstand their playtime. Choose toys that are durable and made of high-quality materials. Toys that fall apart quickly can be dangerous for your cat, as they may swallow small pieces.

Age and Personality

When choosing toys for your cat, consider their age and personality. Kittens have different needs than senior cats, and some cats may prefer certain types of toys over others. For example, some cats may prefer toys that mimic the movements of prey, such as mice or birds, while others may prefer toys that they can chase or swat.

Variety

Providing a variety of toys and accessories can help keep your cat engaged and prevent boredom. You can rotate your cat's toys every few days to keep them interested. You can also provide different types of toys, such as balls, puzzle feeders, wand toys, and scratching posts.

Conclusion

In conclusion, creating a stimulating environment for your cat is essential for their physical and mental health. Providing vertical space, hiding spots, and windows can help create a stimulating environment for your cat. Interactive toys, scratching posts, and playtime can provide mental and physical stimulation. When choosing toys and accessories for your cat, consider their safety, durability, age, and personality. Providing a variety of toys and accessories can help keep your cat engaged and prevent boredom. By following these tips, you can help create a healthy and enriching environment for your feline friend.

Chapter 6: Health and Safety Considerations

Training a cat can be a rewarding experience for both the owner and the pet. However, before beginning any training sessions, it is important to ensure the health and safety of your cat. In this chapter, we will discuss the key factors to consider when training your cat, including making sure your cat is healthy enough for training, keeping your cat safe during training, and preventing stress and anxiety in your cat.

Making Sure Your Cat is Healthy Enough for Training

Before beginning any training, it is important to ensure that your cat is healthy enough for training. A visit to the vet is a good idea, especially if you are unsure about your cat's health. Your vet can conduct a physical examination and make sure your cat is up to date on all vaccinations. Additionally, your vet can provide guidance on any specific training needs your cat may have based on their age, breed, or any underlying medical conditions.

During the vet visit, you should discuss any concerns you may have about your cat's health. For example, if your cat has a history of respiratory issues or is prone to ear infections, you will want to take this into account when planning training sessions. Your vet may recommend certain training techniques or equipment to avoid exacerbating any pre-existing health conditions.

It is also important to monitor your cat's health throughout the training process. Pay attention to your cat's eating and drinking habits, as well as their litter box usage. If you notice any changes in your cat's behavior or health, it may be necessary to pause or modify training until you can consult with your vet.

Keeping Your Cat Safe During Training

Training can be an exciting time for both you and your cat, but it is important to remember that it can also be risky. As you work on training your cat, you should take steps to ensure their safety. Here are a few things to keep in mind:

Choose a safe location: When training your cat, choose a safe location that is free of hazards. Make sure that the area is enclosed, so your cat cannot escape or become lost. Also, remove any items that could pose a danger to your cat, such as sharp objects or toxic substances.

Supervise your cat: Always supervise your cat during training sessions. Never leave your cat unattended, especially if you are using equipment like leashes or harnesses.

Use proper equipment: When using equipment like leashes or harnesses, make sure it is properly fitted and in good condition. If the equipment is too loose, your cat may be able to slip out of it. If it is too tight, it can cause discomfort or injury.

Avoid physical punishment: Never physically punish your cat during training. This can cause your cat to become fearful or aggressive, and can damage your relationship with your pet.

Consider a cat-safe environment: In some cases, it may be necessary to create a cat-safe environment in your home. This could involve using baby gates to block off certain areas or creating a "safe room" for your cat to retreat to when they need a break from training.

Preventing Stress and Anxiety in Your Cat

Cats are sensitive creatures, and they can easily become stressed or anxious during training. To prevent this from happening, there are several steps you can take:

Use positive reinforcement: Positive reinforcement is the most effective way to train a cat. Use treats, praise, and affection to reward good behavior. This will help your cat associate training with positive experiences.

Keep training sessions short: Cats have short attention spans, and they can become bored or frustrated quickly. Keep training sessions short, ideally 10-15 minutes at a time.

Take breaks: If your cat seems stressed or overwhelmed, take a break from training.

This will give your cat a chance to relax and reset, and will help prevent stress and anxiety from building up.

Avoid overstimulation: Avoid overstimulating your cat during training. Too much noise or activity can be overwhelming for your cat, causing stress and anxiety. Train in a quiet, calm environment, and avoid any unnecessary distractions.

Understand your cat's body language: Cats communicate through their body language, and it is important to understand what your cat is telling you. If your cat is showing signs of stress or anxiety, such as flattened ears, a puffed-up tail, or hissing, it is time to take a break from training.

Offer plenty of play and exercise: Play and exercise are important for your cat's mental and physical health. Make sure your cat is getting enough playtime and exercise outside of training sessions. This will help reduce stress and anxiety, and will make training more effective.

Use calming aids if necessary: If your cat is particularly anxious, you may need to use calming aids to help them relax. There are a variety of natural remedies, such as pheromone sprays or herbal supplements, that can help calm your cat during training.

Conclusion

Training a cat can be a rewarding experience, but it is important to keep your cat's health and safety in mind. By making sure your cat is healthy enough for training, keeping them safe during training, and preventing stress and anxiety, you can ensure a positive training experience for both you and your cat. Remember to always use positive reinforcement, keep training sessions short, and take breaks as needed. With patience and consistency, you can train your cat to be a well-behaved and happy companion.

Chapter7: Conclusion

Congratulations on making it to the conclusion of this book on how to train your cat! By now, you should have a good understanding of the benefits of cat training, the natural behavior of cats, and various training techniques that you can use to train your cat.

In this conclusion, we will take a look at the key points that were covered in the book and provide some encouragement for you to continue training your cat and improving your bond with them.

Firstly, we looked at the benefits of cat training. Training your cat can help to reduce behavioral problems, such as aggression, scratching furniture, or litter box issues. It can also improve the bond between you and your cat, as well as provide mental and physical stimulation for your furry friend.

We also addressed some of the common misconceptions about cat training. Many people believe that cats cannot be trained, but this is simply not true. Cats are intelligent animals that can learn a variety of behaviors through positive reinforcement.

The principles of positive reinforcement were discussed in detail, as they are the foundation of successful cat training. Positive reinforcement involves rewarding your cat for good behavior, which encourages them to repeat the behavior in the future. It is important to use treats, praise, and affection to reinforce good behavior, rather than punishment or scolding.

Next, we looked at the natural behavior of cats and how to understand their body language and vocalization. This is important for successful training, as it allows you to communicate effectively with your cat and understand their needs and desires.

Basic training techniques were covered, such as teaching your cat to come when called, litter box training, and training your cat to use a scratching post. These are essential behaviors that all cats should know and can be taught through positive reinforcement.

We also covered more advanced training techniques, such as clicker training, teaching your cat to walk on a leash, and training your cat to perform tricks. These behaviors are not essential, but they can be fun and provide additional mental and physical stimulation for your cat.

Dealing with behavioral problems is an important part of cat training, and we discussed some common issues, such as aggression, scratching furniture, and litter box issues. These behaviors can be frustrating for cat owners, but they can be addressed through positive reinforcement and environmental enrichment.

Environmental enrichment for cats was also covered, which involves creating a stimulating environment for your cat and providing mental and physical stimulation. This can be achieved through toys, scratching posts, and providing opportunities for your cat to hunt and play.

Finally, we addressed health and safety considerations, such as making sure your cat is healthy enough for training and keeping your cat safe during training. It is also important to prevent stress and anxiety in your cat, which can be achieved through positive reinforcement and providing a comfortable and stimulating environment.

In conclusion, training your cat can provide numerous benefits, including reducing behavioral problems, improving the bond between you and your cat, and providing mental and physical stimulation. Positive reinforcement is the key to successful cat training, and a variety of training techniques can be used to teach your cat essential behaviors and fun tricks.

We encourage you to continue training your cat and improving your bond with them. Remember to be patient, use positive reinforcement, and provide a stimulating environment for your furry friend. With time and effort, you can train your cat to be a well-behaved and happy companion. Thank you for reading this book and good luck with your cat training journey!

Printed in Great Britain
by Amazon